CREATIVE Godparenting

Catherine A. H. Walker

Liguori

Imprimi Potest:
Thomas D. Picton, CSsR
Provincial, Denver Province
The Redemptorists

ISBN 978-0-7648-1570-6
© 2007, Liguori Publications
To order, call 800-325-9521, or visit Liguori.org.

All rights reserved. No part of this pamphlet may be reproduced, stored in a retrieval system, or transmitted without the written permission of Liguori Publications.

Scripture quotations are from the *New Revised Standard Version of the Bible,* © 1989 by the Division of Christian Education of the National Council of Churches of Christ in the USA. Used with permission. All rights reserved.

Excerpts from the English translation of the *Catechism of the Catholic Church* for use in the United States of America, © 1993, United States Conference of Catholic Bishops, Inc. Libreria Editrice Vaticana. Used with permission.

Liguori Publications, a nonprofit corporation, is an apostolate of the Redemptorists. To learn more about the Redemptorists, visit Redemptorists.com.

Cover design: Wendy Barnes • Cover image: Digital Vision

Printed in the United States of America
24 23 22 21 20 / 8 7 6 5 4

Introduction

Baptism is the sacrament of faith. But faith needs the community of believers...The catechumen or the godparent is asked: "What do you ask of God's Church?" The response is: "Faith!"

CATECHISM OF THE CATHOLIC CHURCH, 1253

When my father grew up on the South Side of Chicago in the 1950s, his first cousins lived two doors down from him. Almost everyone in his family lived within walking distance and certainly within a quick bus ride. No one lived out of town, let alone in another state or country.

When Aunt Nan and Uncle Stanley became my father's godparents, everyone knew how they would stay in touch. They came to dinner, frequently attended Mass with the family (they belonged to the same parish, after all), and attended school functions and parish celebrations. They were present for my father's first Communion, the first time he served as an altar boy, and his confirmation.

Times have changed. I have three siblings. I am in Minnesota, my sister is in North Carolina, and one brother is in New York and the other in Illinois. We remain close and talk regularly via e-mail and telephone, but we manage to gather together only once or twice each year. Meanwhile, my husband's brother and sister live in different parts of Iowa, and he has other relatives in Illinois and Texas.

My children know their aunts and uncles through stories, photos, and telephone calls. They have a degree of shyness to overcome when we visit these relatives before they are comfortable with them.

I think many present-day families with young children have similar experiences. Our modern, mobile age has advantages, but we have lost the closeness that physical proximity fosters within families. How are children to develop close relationships with people they see only rarely?

I was faced with these issues when, six years ago, I was asked to be a godparent by some very close friends. Delighted, honored, and overwhelmed, I accepted. But I had to start thinking. My goddaughter lives in Chicago; I am in Minneapolis. How could I build a relationship with her across that distance? How could I assist her parents in her spiritual growth, as a godparent agrees to do?

You Are a Godparent! Now What?

For the grace of Baptism to unfold, the parents' help is important. So too is the role of the godfather and godmother, who must be firm believers, able and ready to help the newly baptized—child or adult—on the road of Christian life. Their task is a truly ecclesial function (officium).

CATECHISM OF THE CATHOLIC CHURCH, 1255

A godparent is "able and ready to help...on the road of Christian life." This is an honor and an awesome responsibility. How do we fulfill it?

If you are lucky, you live close to your godchild. You can begin to be a part of his or her life by seeing the family often and attending all the important events. If you do not live in the same area, you will need to plan more carefully.

Use the suggestions in this pamphlet as jumping-off points to come up with your own ideas for developing a special relationship with your godchild. No one can do all the projects in this pamphlet—I certainly haven't done all of them for my own godchildren. But there should be enough different ideas to help you. This pamphlet is a tool for you to use from the time you become a godparent and throughout your lives together.

Praying for Your Godchild

Praying for your godchild is a duty you accepted when you agreed to be a godparent. Put a picture of your godchild in a prominent place: tape a small photo on your computer monitor, above the kitchen sink, and so on. Seeing it daily will remind you to pray for him or her.

When praying, thank God you have been chosen for this incredible role and for the blessings he has bestowed on your godchild. Ask for the grace and wisdom to fulfill your responsibility. Ask God to keep your godchild physically and spiritually safe. Ask God to guide you as you help your godchild realize and fulfill his or her vocation in life.

I often think of my godchildren when I say the Apostles' Creed, remembering that I professed this vow for them in the sacrament of baptism. I also frequently say a *Memorare* for each of them, petitioning our Blessed Mother to take each under her care.

Getting to Know Your Godchild

Talk to your godchild's parents often to find out more about his or her daily life. Before talking with a toddler or preschooler on the telephone, ask the parents what the child has done recently. Has he or she been to the zoo, helped in the garden, watched a new video? Then ask the child some specific questions. Most five-year-olds will respond to the question "What have you been doing?" with "Umm...." But if you say, "I hear you walked to the park this afternoon. How many times did you go down the slide?" you have a much better chance of starting a conversation.

Ask your godchild to write to you. Send a gift of preaddressed, stamped envelopes.

Personalized stationery (done inexpensively on your computer) will be appreciated by an older child. For younger ones, ask the parents if they will send you artwork or other keepsakes.

Projects to Do Together

If you are planning a project with or for your godchild, *discuss it with his or her parents first!* Every family has its own constraints on time, money, transportation, resources, and talent. Something that seems easy and fun to you—even something you do with your own children—may be tedious and difficult for another family.

Find out what time your godchild's family says their morning and evening prayers. Tell the child you will try to pray at the same time.

Purchase two good Catholic calendars that include the daily Mass readings. Keep one and send the other to an older godchild; ask him or her to read along with you.

Talk to your godchild about the works of penance you are planning for Advent or Lent. Perhaps you can choose something similar: both giving up sweets, saying the Chaplet of Divine Mercy each day, and so on.

Talk to your godchild about a person or cause that needs prayers. It could be personal (a sick friend, vocation guidance) or more global (the pro-life movement, worldwide vocations). Compose a prayer together and pray it regularly.

Ask your godchild to perform a service along with you. Some examples:

- Walk up and down your block and pick up trash.
- Help a neighbor rake autumn leaves.
- Donate a toy to a homeless shelter.
- Donate groceries to a food pantry.
- Visit a nursing home.
- Save loose change for a mission during Lent.

When You Are Together

Make the most of the time you're physically with your godchild, whether you visit once a week or once a year.

When you visit, ask if you can take your godchild to daily Mass, just the two of you, maybe with a special breakfast or other treat afterward. Attend Sunday Mass with the family if you have the chance.

Many parishes hold baptisms during one particular Mass every month. If you can, take your godchild. When the congregation repeats the baptismal vows, you will be taking these vows together—the same vows you took at the child's own baptism. You can do the same thing at the Easter Vigil (Holy Saturday) celebration. What a powerful experience!

You can also accompany your godchild to the sacrament of reconciliation.

Call or visit on the anniversary of the child's baptism. Try to take him or her out for a special lunch or dinner. You could also bring a small gift. Remind your godchild that you pray for him or her, and ask the child to pray for you as well.

Show your godchild how much you support and celebrate his or her life in the Church. Be there for May Processions, Advent programs, and so forth, when you can. If your godchild is an altar server, try to attend a Mass he or she serves at.

Be involved in your godchild's sacramental preparation. Ask about what he or she is learning while preparing for first reconciliation, first Communion, or confirmation (and, one day, perhaps marriage or holy orders). Prepare a special gift or remembrance: can you give a special rosary or prayer book? sew a veil? bake the cake for the celebration? Attend the event if you possibly can. Whether or not you can be physically present, write a heartfelt note to your godchild.

Spend time talking and listening, learning about your godchild, and enjoying one another's company. Participate in activities you both enjoy.

Writing to Your Godchild

Write a letter every month to your godchild. A real, honest-to-goodness letter through the mail, with a stamp and everything.

Regular letters get you in the habit of thinking of and praying for your godchild. Your godchild will grow to anticipate your letters—and get in the habit of thinking of and praying for you.

Even in this high-tech age of e-mails and phone calls, everyone gets excited when "real" mail arrives.

What Should You Write About?

You may be afraid you will run out of ideas for letter topics. Or that you will be unable to think of things a child will find interesting or relevant. Or that your knowledge of the faith is not well developed enough for you to know what is appropriate.

The following ideas will jog your imagination and get you thinking along the right lines. Be confident that as you develop a relationship with your godchild, you will know him or her well enough to write interesting letters.

As far as your knowledge of the faith goes, committing to this deep relationship will prove a blessing to you as well. Your first letters will be simple, childlike things. As the child grows, your letters will become more mature and your faith will deepen as well.

These letters should be chatty and personal—they're not lectures. Write about your personal life and talk about how your faith impacts, and is impacted by, daily events. Share stories and ask about recent events in the child's life.

Saints

Your letters and interactions should show your godchild the duty we have to incorporate our faith into our work—and the dignity and fulfillment we find when we do so. A good book about the saints is an invaluable resource for any godparent. Find ways to incorporate the lives of the saints into your letters and talks. Write about the patron saint of your profession—whether you are a nurse, engineer, or mother. Find out what profession your godchild is currently interested in—this could change from truck driver to doctor to ballerina to plumber. Tell the child about the patron saint of each profession as his or her interests change.

When your godchild is preparing for an important test, tell him or her about the patron saints of scholars: Saint Bridgid of Ireland and Saint Thomas Aquinas. Saint Joseph of

Cupertino is the patron saint of examinees. Ask about your godchild's favorite subjects at school and find the patron saints related to those subjects. The patron saint of public education is Saint Martin de Porres.

If your godchild gets a new pet, remind him or her that Saint Francis is the patron of all animals. Some animals are associated with other saints as well.

If your godchild is going to the doctor or has been ill lately, you could mention Saint Luke—the patron saint of doctors. Saint Genevieve is the patron saint of fevers. Many other ailments are associated with a specific saint.

If your godchild is expecting a new brother or sister, talk about the patron saints of babies: Holy Innocents, Maximus, Nicholas of Tolentino, and Philip of Zell. Ask your godchild to pray for his or her mother; the patron saints of expectant mothers are Gerard Majella and Raymond Nonnatus.

Is your godchild going on a trip? Saint Joseph of Cupertino is also the patron saint of flying. The patron saints of travelers are Raphael the Archangel, Nicholas of Myra, Anthony of Padua, Christopher, and Joseph.

Is a relative getting married? The patron saint of marriage is Saint John Francis Regis.

Catholic Doctrine

The Church in this world is the sacrament of salvation, the sign and the instrument of the communion of God and men.

CATECHISM OF THE CATHOLIC CHURCH, 780

Your letters, talks, and activities should reinforce various aspects of the Faith. Take several months and do a running theme; for example, say prayers and do activities for each of the seven corporal works of mercy, focusing on one every month.

Themes could include
- Ten Commandments
- Sacraments
- Theological virtues: faith, hope, and charity
- Cardinal virtues: prudence, justice, fortitude, and temperance
- Corporal works of mercy: feed the hungry, give drink to the thirsty, clothe the naked, visit the imprisoned, shelter the homeless, visit the sick, and bury the dead
- Spiritual works of mercy: admonish the sinner, instruct the ignorant, counsel the doubtful, comfort the sorrowful, bear wrongs patiently, forgive all injuries, and pray for the living and the dead
- Gifts of the Holy Spirit: wisdom, understanding, knowledge, right judgment (counsel), courage (fortitude), reverence (piety), and wonder and awe in the presence of God (fear of the Lord)
- A Marian feast for each month

The Catholic Calendar

Every month, you can help yourself write by choosing a topic relevant to the time of year. It is easy to find holy cards and books, for example, that relate to a certain saint or liturgical season. A Saint Nicholas card in December, for example, or a children's book on the rosary for May make appropriate seasonal gifts.

Be sure you relate faith to the everyday occurrences everyone experiences and celebrates. Show your godchild that God, faith, and spirituality are not "other" objects that get pulled out only for church and holidays. In the spring, for example, send a gardener's prayer. When school starts, send some "God Loves Me!" stickers to put on a pencil box.

Helpful Hints

- Pray before you write. Ask for inspiration from the Holy Spirit.
- Your letters are trying to promote faith formation and spirituality. But be yourself. When writing and speaking to your godchild, use *your* voice, *your* mannerisms, *your* speech. You will sound phony if you use one set of mannerisms for everyday conversation and another for religious talk.
- Don't be preachy. These are letters, after all; you're not composing a tutorial.
- Don't just stuff a holy card in an envelope and mail it. Always include a note. Even if you only have time to write a few sentences, do so.
- Make the mechanics of the process automatic and easy. Preaddress a number of envelopes or print out a sheet of labels. Keep

your materials together and accessible. For example, I keep my envelopes in the folder where I file my bills. When I sit down once a month to write out checks, my godchild supplies are there as well.
- Humor is appropriate! Tell a frustrated preteen complaining about her chore load you will ask Saint Zita, the patron saint of maids, to pray for her.

The Godparent Book

What is a Godparent Book? It is a collection of the letters and items you've sent your godchild over the years. It will become a personal and special book for your godchild.

Often we don't know what to do with letters and cards people send us. Too often they end up stuffed in a dusty box that may get dragged out every few years to crowd in more cards. Help your godchild collect your letters and keep them handy. The Godparent Book can also hold the holy cards you've sent.

Children love collections, as is evidenced by periodic crazes—action figures, trading cards, popular toys, and so on. Sending a monthly letter builds a unique collection to help your godchild along life's spiritual journey—years of notes from you to treasure. You will also build a relationship and form memories.

Getting Started

You will need the following supplies for a Godparent Book:

- A three-ring binder that is sturdy but not overly large. Small arms and hands will have trouble with a three-inch, heavy-duty binder. Get a smaller one. When it fills up, send another.
- Clear sheet protectors to hold your letters and cards. You can get archival-quality sheet protectors at an office supply store or discount store. They have three holes to fit in a three-ring binder and are big enough to hold an 8½ x 11–inch sheet of paper.
- Trading-card pages to hold holy cards. Trading-card pages have three holes for binders and nine pockets. Holy cards are

generally the same width but about one-fourth–inch longer than standard-sized trading cards. Still, the pockets will hold holy cards with minimal overlap, especially if you stagger them. You could buy pocket photo sheets instead of trading-card sheets, but photo sheets generally have an opaque back and only one side of the card can be seen.
- One or two items to begin the Godparent Book. Choose a guardian-angel holy card, a card of the child's patron saint, some stickers to decorate the book (parents or older siblings can do this for infants), and so on. This will make a nice beginning to the book, and parents will see what you will be doing.

Assemble the book by putting several pages of the sheet protectors and trading-card pages in the binder. Tuck in the first items.

Now, write a letter to the parents. Be sure to thank them for the honor they have bestowed on you. Explain the Godparent Book and tell them you will be sending monthly letters to put in it. Ask them to keep the book updated. If you like, include a small booklet of prayers for mothers or fathers or a book on family spirituality.

Most important, write a letter telling your godchild how happy you are to be chosen to help him or her learn about God.

Sample Letter

Dear Adriana:

Happy one-month birthday (almost)! I am so glad you have arrived and am very excited and anxious to meet you for the first time in a few weeks. You see, we live pretty far away from each other and will not be able to visit very often.

I was so pleased and proud when your mama and daddy asked me to be your godmother that I cried. Being your godmother means it is my job to help your parents teach you about God and his great love for you. That is an important job, a hard one, and it is even harder for me because I live so far away from you.

I have been thinking about some ways we can get to know each other so I can share with you just how important you are and how much God loves you. I want to try some different things, but we'll start with this:

In this package is a purple notebook. Purple is a good color to remind us about God because purple is the color of kings and God is our Heavenly King. Inside the notebook are some pocket pages. Every month I am going to send you a note and something for this book. The note will help you remember me, and the little something will help you learn about God. Holy cards will fit in the little pockets, and booklets and prayers will fit in the bigger pockets. Sometimes I will send you things to decorate your notebook too. (I put some stickers on it already, just to get you started.)

You are very little now, and there isn't much in this book. But by the time you are old enough to look through it and use it, there will be enough to keep you interested. And you can look forward to getting something to add every month.

I hope this book will be a special reminder for you of God and of me. You should know I pray for you every day. Every single day! I hope when you are older you will pray for me too. God especially listens to the prayers of children, and I need all the help I can get.

Take care, sweet one, and be well. I will meet you soon.

What to Send

In addition to your letters, the following things could be included in the Godparent Book:

- Holy cards. Try to send several holy cards in the first few years. They will fill the book quickly with images and color, which will be very impressive to a young child.
- Prayers you have typed or handwritten.
- Newspaper and magazine clippings your godchild will find helpful or interesting on his or her own spiritual path.

Your godchild will come to see the Godparent Book as a work in progress, slowly growing, just like his or her relationship with God.

Gifts for Your Godchild

In many ways, this is the least important part of this pamphlet. Too often, adults try to build relationships with children by showering them with unnecessary material gifts. Expense is not an indication of the love that goes into choosing and presenting a gift. On the other hand, gift-giving from the heart is a very beautiful thing.

Our culture associates gifts with birthdays and the December holidays. As a godparent, however, you can give gifts to further your godchild's faith. Your role is to help develop the child's Christian life. Deepen that special relationship by avoiding secular gifts. Most American children have more dolls, trucks, and forgettable plastic junk than they can ever play with.

Give a significant gift to commemorate the anniversary of the child's baptism rather than on his or her birthday. He or she will probably celebrate with a birthday party every year. As a godparent, you can emphasize the date the child entered the family of God.

You can also celebrate the child's name day: the feast day of his or her patron saint.

Easter gifts don't have to be stuffed bunnies and candy eggs (which your godchild will probably have plenty of anyway). A holy card or a small book about the resurrection will better illuminate the joy of the Church's greatest feast.

What Kind of Gifts?

Children, even very small children, should have access to religious objects every day; it is a mistake to split their lives into "regular time" and "religious time." Encourage your godchild's parents to let him or her handle and use religious objects. Plastic rosaries, unbreakable statues, and other objects should be part of the child's daily life.

But children should be taught to treat religious objects with respect. All it takes is some gentle instruction. "Look, Deborah, this is the way to hold a rosary." "Tom, let's be nice to Baby Jesus. Let's cuddle him and sing him a song." Rosaries should not be used as collars for stuffed animals, and prayer cards should not be folded into paper airplanes.

A nice gift would be a storage box for religious objects so they won't be thrown in the toy box with the dolls and trucks.

When your godchild is old enough, you can have objects blessed before you send them. Make sure the child and parents know you have done this. You may not want to send blessed objects when the child is a toddler. However, when the child is older, you can take him or her to Mass and get a priest to bless the objects afterward. It can be a special event.

Homemade Gifts

Nothing will mean more to your godchild than something you made yourself. When a toddler asks mommy to draw a picture of a horse, the child is always delighted with the results—even if the horse looks like nothing as much as a potato with scraggly sprouts for limbs.

- If you draw or paint: make a sketch of your church or paint a small portrait of the Blessed Mother.
- If you do needlecraft: make a Bible cover, crochet a cross-shaped bookmark, or sew a special "church bag" to carry books to Mass.
- If you do woodwork: make a set of bookends, a box to keep rosaries in, a picture frame for a special photo or holy card.

- If you scrapbook: make a scrapbook of your godchild's baptism or another special day.
- If you stamp: design the stationery/cards for your monthly letters. Make a set of cards for your godchild's use.
- If you write: compose a poem or a song. Anyone can compose a special, personal prayer. Type it on fancy paper, and tell your godchild it is the prayer you will be saying for him or her.
- If you sing: record yourself singing some hymns. If you don't like to sing, record yourself saying your nightly prayers or the rosary. Read aloud a Bible story or a saint story. Believe me—this will be played over and over again.

Intangible Gifts

Help your godchild learn to appreciate intangible gifts by giving them often. When you donate to missions, for example, do so in honor of your godchild and send the thank you note to him or her.

Spend an hour at eucharistic adoration for your godchild. Maybe you can coordinate with the parents so you and your godchild will be adoring at the same time—maybe only ten or fifteen minutes for a young child. What a way to unite across the miles!

Material Gifts

Every Catholic child over four years of age should have a rosary. Do not leave young children alone with anything they can wrap around their necks; it only takes a few seconds to be strangled. Be sure the child is supervised when he or she handles a rosary.

For very young children, rosaries with large wooden beads are strung on a strong nylon cord. These are very difficult for a toddler to break. Preschoolers could use a nearly unbreakable (and very inexpensive) rosary made of bright plastic molded onto strong cord. Even an older child who can handle a fancier rosary should have one of these for a backup.

Wait until the parents think your godchild is old enough before you buy rosaries of linked chain. Even a responsible, careful child can accidentally yank these too hard or get them caught on things. Wait until the child is old enough before buying an expensive rosary. If you give an expensive rosary for first Communion, ask the parents to keep it at home for family prayer—a rosary with less emotional value can be sent to school.

Every child should have an age-appropriate Bible: board-book picture Bibles for toddlers, a Bible that uses simple sentences for preschoolers, and so on. Christian bookstores have large selections of children's Bibles. Unless you are buying a Bible in a Catholic bookstore, however, look it over carefully before purchasing. Picture books won't vary too much from Catholic doctrine because of their simplicity. But even Bibles aimed at preschoolers can have omissions if they were written for a Protestant audience.

For example, I have a nice children's Bible for early readers that breaks the Bible into 365 short passages. I liked the idea that I could read one or two pieces to my very young daughter every evening and cover the main biblical stories. When reading the passages on the Last Supper, however, I found the text completely omitted Jesus' words "This is my body" and "This is my blood." The sacrament Jesus instituted at the Last Supper was completely ignored. I pulled out my adult

Bible and read these verses with my daughter. To avoid problems like this, purchase Bibles intended for Catholic children.

A number of delightful books on the saints have been developed for all ages. Make sure your godchild has some that are appropriate for his or her age and interests. A book about his or her patron saint should certainly be part of the collection.

Your godchild should also have a prayer book that includes the essential Catholic prayers: the Our Father, Hail Mary, Glory Be, Apostles' Creed, and so on. Many children's books also include short, simple prayers pertinent to a child's life. Many include prayer topics such as "When I'm Scared" or "I'm Sorry, God" and familiarize the child with the concept of prayer as conversation with God.

Every adult Catholic should have a *Catechism of the Catholic Church*. If your godchild's family does not have one, give one as a family present. When your godchild reaches the teen years, give him or her a personal copy.

Inexpensive Gifts

- Seeds are a nice, inexpensive gift for early spring. Your godchild can plant them indoors and watch them grow. Send bulbs in the fall that can be enjoyed in the spring. Be sure to talk about these as symbols of the resurrection; what looks dead returns beautifully, wondrously to life.
- Laminated holy cards are very inexpensive. Some bookstores give a discount on holy cards if you purchase a certain number. Buy a handful, punch a hole in the corner, and put them on a sturdy key ring. These make wonderful quiet toys for younger children to handle during Mass.
- Small tokens from a religious bookstore—a a cross for the bedroom, a Holy Spirit pin,

plastic rosaries—make wonderful gifts.
- Buy a coloring book of saints; you could send one page at a time with your monthly letter.
- Buy a package of stickers and send one sheet at a time. Some bookstores have rolls of stickers for sale. You can also buy them individually.
- Check out your parish literature rack for prayer books and other relevant materials; make sure to put an appropriate donation in the donation box.
- You can find Catholic children's websites and print puzzles, pictures, and stories to send to your godchild. Make sure you are not violating usage agreements by doing this. Generally, you have not violated copyright laws if you print one copy of a web page for personal, noncommercial use.

Other Ideas

- Religious-music CDs are a nice gift. Bookends for your godchild's special shelf of religious books would also be appropriate.
- Suggest a special dinner on the anniversary of your godchild's baptism. Offer to pay for the family to go if you cannot attend yourself.
- A Nativity set is an excellent gift that can span several years of your godchild's life. Choose a good-quality Nativity set, and give the child one piece each year. By the time he or she is an adult, the set will be a wonderful reminder of you during the holidays.
- A Nativity set made of an unbreakable material will be appreciated by a young child—and his or her parents. A number of lovely sets use a nearly indestructible resin or durable plastic. Avoid fancy porcelain or

ceramic sets; those beautiful figures will be admired from a high shelf but will never mean as much to the child as the set he or she can handle.
- Larger gifts could include a week at a Catholic day camp or a teen-retreat weekend.

Go and Spread the Good News!

"Go therefore and make disciples of all nations, baptizing them in the name of the Father and of the Son and of the Holy Spirit, and teaching them to obey everything that I have commanded you. And remember, I am with you always, to the end of the age."

MATTHEW 28:19–20

That is a better summary to the calling of being a godparent than I could come up with myself. I hope you've taken some practical help and creative ideas from this pamphlet. God bless you and your godchild.

Notes

Use the following pages for notes and ideas for your own godchild.

Praying for Your Godchild

_____

_____

_____

_____

Projects With Your Godchild

_____

_____

_____

_____

Writing to Your Godchild

_____

_____

_____

_____

The Godparent Book

_____

_____

_____

_____

Gifts for Your Godchild

_____

_____

_____

_____